I0022333

Robert Awde

Jubilee

Patriotic and other Poems

Robert Awde

Jubilee
Patriotic and other Poems

ISBN/EAN: 9783337307110

Printed in Europe, USA, Canada, Australia, Japan

Cover: Foto ©Thomas Meinert / pixelio.de

More available books at **www.hansebooks.com**

JUBILEE, PATRIOTIC,

AND OTHER POEMS.

BY

ROBERT AWDE.

TORONTO:

WILLIAM BRIGGS, 78 & 80 KING STREET EAST.

MONTREAL: C. W. COATES.   HALIFAX: S. F. HUESTIS.

1887.

TO

MY WIFE,

MY QUEEN,

AND

MY FELLOW-COUNTRYMEN

THESE POEMS ARE

RESPECTFULLY INSCRIBED.

THE AUTHOR.

PREFACE.

"O THAT mine enemy would write a book!" Whether the writer of this passage was also a writer of reviews I know not; but doubtless many an author has been assailed when such an opportunity was afforded to his readers. And though such an ordeal is not pleasant to face, yet the humble author before you is not deterred by such apprehensions. He is, however, considerably embarrassed to make such a selection from recent productions as will meet with the appreciation of his fellow-countrymen, and especially his fellow-subjects.

It is, however, impossible to feel confident and buoyant in the face of the experience of Canadian poets who have ventured into print. The poor success they have met with is not owing altogether to their productions. It may be they did not meet with the enthusiastic reception they deserved; or it may be the poetic culture of their readers was far beyond their best efforts. It could not be that the soul of Young Canada is sordid and low. Is it not to be found rather in the fact that our educational institutions have passed over home talent in their gifts, prizes, and reading selections, and unconsciously defeated one of the chief objects of our educational system—the cultivation of patriotism? Whatever the cause, the unpleasant facts remain, and on this account the author has timidly ventured to offer this very small book, rather than risk the uncertainties attending the issue of a volume of five hundred pages.

Further, he cannot claim the indulgence usually accorded

to first efforts, having published in London, in 1865, a small volume of poems and songs, which sold rapidly at 3/6. How that work was received the following brief extracts from the reviews of that day will show :—

The *Atheneum* says : " From a perusal of the poems and songs under notice we can conscientiously say that Robert Awde's name fully deserves to be associated with those of the individuals above named. . . . . Of the poems we can say that a high moral and religious tone pervades them throughout, and many remind us of Heber's best writings." The Brighton *Gazette* says : " Our author is as pure, pleasing, and original in his conceptions as he is strict in his rhythm. . . . . We can commend most favourably this little work as a whole." The *News of the World* says : " We are reminded occasionally, as we go through this little volume, of the lyrics of the second Charles' days. . . . . We have read a great deal worse poetry that has been published with more pretension." The *Sun* says : " This little volume of Robert Awde's is well worthy of a respectful examination." The *Morning News* says : " The volume before us contains sufficient indications of the ' divine afflatus ' to rank Mr. Awde among the poets."

Others might be quoted, and those at greater length, but modesty forbids; these are given only to excite your curiosity and if possible awaken an interest in the volume before you. Should it do so, and lead to a kindly reception of this fragment of his productions, the author will feel encouraged to launch out and publish something much larger.

I am, my dear reader,

Your humble servant,

ROBERT AWDE.

TORONTO, *June, 1887.*

JUBILEE, PATRIOTIC,

AND OTHER POEMS.

———•◦•———

Her Majesty's Jubilee.

I.

EMPRESS AND QUEEN! of thee shall poets sing
When other themes, like gold mines of Peru,
Have yielded all, and all-forsaken lie.
Thou to their Muse shalt be as budding Spring,
With zephyrs laden and with smiles profuse.
Surcharged with life and wealth of flowers untold,
Shalt win from them a fruitage passing fair.
Thy life, full-orbed, in lustrous beauty shines,
And forms a subject worthy of their songs.
Peerless in all that makes a woman great,
We hail thee Empress! and enthrone thee such,
To reign, by right, our most beloved Queen!

II.

For fifty years the sceptre in thy hands
Has been a blessing, like to Aaron's rod.

to first efforts, having published in London, in 1865, a small volume of poems and songs, which sold rapidly at 3/6. How that work was received the following brief extracts from the reviews of that day will show :—

The *Atheneum* says : "From a perusal of the poems and songs under notice we can conscientiously say that Robert Awde's name fully deserves to be associated with those of the individuals above named. . . . . Of the poems we can say that a high moral and religious tone pervades them throughout, and many remind us of Heber's best writings." The Brighton *Gazette* says : "Our author is as pure, pleasing, and original in his conceptions as he is strict in his rhythm. . . . . We can commend most favourably this little work as a whole." The *News of the World* says : "We are reminded occasionally, as we go through this little volume, of the lyrics of the second Charles' days. . . . . We have read a great deal worse poetry that has been published with more pretension." The *Sun* says : "This little volume of Robert Awde's is well worthy of a respectful examination." The *Morning News* says : "The volume before us contains sufficient indications of the 'divine afflatus' to rank Mr. Awde among the poets."

Others might be quoted, and those at greater length, but modesty forbids; these are given only to excite your curiosity and if possible awaken an interest in the volume before you. Should it do so, and lead to a kindly reception of this fragment of his productions, the author will feel encouraged to launch out and publish something much larger.

I am, my dear reader,
Your humble servant,
ROBERT AWDE.

TORONTO, *June, 1887.*

Jubilee, Patriotic,

AND OTHER POEMS.

Her Majesty's Jubilee.

I.

EMPRESS AND QUEEN! of thee shall poets sing
When other themes, like gold mines of Peru,
Have yielded all, and all-forsaken lie.
Thou to their Muse shalt be as budding Spring,
With zephyrs laden and with smiles profuse.
Surcharged with life and wealth of flowers untold,
Shalt win from them a fruitage passing fair.
Thy life, full-orbed, in lustrous beauty shines,
And forms a subject worthy of their songs.
Peerless in all that makes a woman great,
We hail thee Empress! and enthrone thee such,
To reign, by right, our most beloved Queen!

II.

For fifty years the sceptre in thy hands
Has been a blessing, like to Aaron's rod.

New fields have opened through the pathless seas,
And distant lands rejoice to own thy sway.
Thy subjects, multitudinous, arise,
Revere thy name, and think of thee with praise.
Thy merchant princes bring thee wealth from far;
And precious argosies from every zone
Yield freight more varied than in olden time,
When "ships of Tarshish" came to David's son,
With "peacocks, apes, gold, and white iron"—tin.
If his was glory, how much greater thine!

III.

Divinely blessed with more than womanhood,
Thou stand'st to-day, a model mother—Queen.
Thy children, nurtured 'mid domestic bliss,
And taught in all that tends to make them great,
Reflect thy care, the bright example set;
And doubtless shall, as is the wish of all,
Win for themselves, like thee, undying fame.
May He whose right it is to rule e'en kings,
Dispose their hearts by His prevailing grace,
That they, like thee, may walk in Wisdom's ways,
And find the promise theirs—e'en "length of days,
Riches, and honour, and eternal life."

IV.

With joy we hail this year of Jubilee,
And wish for all within our sea-girt isles
God's richest blessings, Wisdom, Love, and Peace;
That these may rest on every head, a crown,

And, like the light, diffusive cast their rays
Alike on thee and on thy subjects all ;
Till judgments, warped by long abuses, yield
To Reason's gentle sway ; and hearts, aflame
With fires unholy, from their ashes rise
To nobler purpose ; feeling all inspired
By mutual love, and every wrong redressed,
To join as one to make our nation great.

V.

No foe shall dare to rouse the " Lion " then ;
The majesty of calm would drive them hence,
And keep them back from fear his might to dare.
So shall our Union and concentred power
Bring greater glory than the blood-wet sword.
So shall the bonds of brotherhood, declared,
Be stronger far than race, or clan, or creed ;
And England, dreaded more than in the past,
Shall onward march, humanity to bless
With Light, and Truth, and Freedom, worth the
      name ;
Hasting the day the nations groan to see,
When, brothers all, they shall learn war no more.

VI.

Of Art the patron thou hast ever been,
Led by the soul so sweetly joined with thine
In efforts grand to raise the nations higher.
His genius won what few had dared to dream,
And twice accomplished, that, but once he saw:

Immortal Prince! Britain still owes to thee
Such meed of praise as most befits thy worth;
A name and place which history will accord—
She never can, nor would she wish, forget,
But deems thy life-work noble, and well done!
Subduing hearts is greater glory far
Than crushing empires with the force of war.

VII.

But how shall words thy finer parts portray,
Thy wealth of love as wife and mother tell;
That soulful sense and reverential awe
Which always marked thee in the public eye.
From very girlhood, when the Lords of State
Announced thee Queen, with true humility
We hear thee say, " I need your Grace's prayers."*
Since then thou aye hast stood to conscience true,
Mildly rebuking statesmen in their haste,
When they would trench upon the holy way;
And deftly pointing, through the preacher's text,†
To duty higher than the State demands.

VIII.

Our peerless Queen and Empress! thee we hail,
And humbly lay our plaudits at thy feet.

* " I beg your Grace to pray for me."

† A certain noble Minister who late on a Saturday night arrived at Windsor with important State papers sought to have the Queen attend to them on Sunday morning. Her Majesty remarked to him, "To-morrow is the Sabbath, my Lord," and also requested him to attend service in the Chapel Royal, after which she would see him. There he heard a sermon preached from a text supplied by the Queen, and was glad to wait till Monday, saying nothing more about the urgency of the case.—" *Queen Victoria," p. 58 (T. F. Ball).*

Thy reign hath blessed us, but not we alone—
The whole world shares the bright, effulgent beams,
Reflecting through thy life and glorious reign
The brighter rays of God's beloved Son!
The sick, the poor, have blessed thee in His name.
Thy tender heart hath yearned o'er widows reft,
And felt assuagement, sharing in their griefs.
' God bless our Queen!" so will we ever pray;
And hold thee high enthroned in all our hearts,
Till thou commit thy sceptre to thy son!

IX.

Hail! Hail! All hail! this year of Jubilee!
Bells! cannons! peoples! speak with loud acclaim;
Let grand memorials rise, our Queen, to thee,
And hold enshrined for aye thy matchless name.

Jubilee Poem.

I.

OUR QUEEN AND EMPRESS! thee we hail
    With feelings deep and tender.
May fervent prayer for thee prevail,
    And God be thy defender.
Through all the fifty years gone by
    His shield each blow has warded;
Thou hast been safe beneath His eye,
    And most securely guarded.

That thou mayest still for us long fill
  Earth's noblest, highest station,
We'll ever pray, and mourn the day
  That takes thee from our nation.

II.

We ask for thine the special grace
  That each like thee may merit,
By virtuous deeds, a higher place
  Than they by birth inherit.
The nation's heart, by these constrained,
  Will yield allegiance ever:
With justice, virtue, love, sustained,
  Thy throne shall stand forever.
Law is not might; but these with right
  Linked to a holy mission—
The people's good—is more than blood,
  Which, felt, brings sweet fruition.

III.

So shall we act a nation's part,
  And feel new life pulsating;
Our patriots ply the statesman's art
  Without disintegrating.
But side by side, in strength arrayed,
  We'll take our true position,
And foreign foes will stand dismayed,
  Nor dare to court collision.
On sea and land, united grand,
  Full armed and self-reliant,

In regal state, a nation great;
   Not proud, nor yet defiant.

IV.

Thy subjects, through thine Empire vast,
   Cry " England's Flag forever,"
As they review the glorious past
   Of noble, high endeavour.
In commerce and in war renowned,
   From days far back and hoary,
We see our fathers, victors crowned,
   Resplendent in their glory.
From every land our Anthem grand
   Has long in prayer ascended,
" God bless our Queen, and intervene
   Whene'er wrong is intended."

V.

Ye cannons ! boom with deafening roar
   Your pithy, prompt orations,
And let them roll from shore to shore,
   In loudest intonations.
Display the fulness of your art,
   Excite the world to wonder ;
Voice, if you can, the nation's heart,
   In plaudits loud as thunder.
Ye mighty hosts that guard our coasts,
   Awake to life and action ;
In flashing flame, and loud acclaim,
   Speak out our satisfaction.

VI.

Ring out, ye bells, a merry peal
　Of silvery song and pleasure !
Express the joy the myriads feel,
　Too deep for words to measure.
In vain musicians labour long
　In efforts at revealing,
Through notes and chords of loftiest song,
　The depths of loyal feeling.
Ye best can tell the thoughts that swell
　The bosom of the nation ;
From belfry choir and graceful spire,
　Peal forth our glad laudation.

VII.

Ye millions, that with beaming eye
　Evince your deep devotion !
Give vent in one harmonious cry,
　And joyousness of motion.
With hip-hurrah, in British style,
　Your hats and 'kerchiefs flying,
Cheer her who gave her brightest smile
　To those in anguish lying.
For she has blessed the sore distressed
　Of every grade and station ;
Her loving deeds all praise exceed,
　And claim our admiration.

VIII.

In fevered ward and hospital,
　In cottar's humble dwelling,

Are souvenirs upon the wall,
   Her acts of kindness telling.
Worn, languid eyes have brighter burned,
   And pallid lips have parted,
In grateful thanks, as she has turned
   To heal the broken-hearted.
Her tears have blent as she has bent
   O'er those reft of defender,
And widow's grief has found relief
   By touch so true, so tender. .

We therefore pray, our Queen, for thee,
And hail thy year of Jubilee!

The Queen's Birthday.

GOD bless our Sovereign Lady, Queen of England's
   wide domain,
Let every heart breathe forth the prayer, " God grant
   she long may reign,"
Beloved by all of every land, but by Canadians most,
As witness now the merry din that rolls from coast to
   coast.

From east to west, around the world, where'er are
   Britain's sons,
Their glad acclaim will mingle with the thunder of
   the guns,

And noble spirits feel the glow of patriotic pride,
As party lines and politics for once are cast aside.

No Whigs or Tories rule to-day, but patriots brave and
  . true,
Whose blood unshed is just as red as foeman ever
    drew;
And should the battle-cloud arise, and Britain need
    our aid,
She'd find this young Dominion prove a true Damas-
    cus blade.

For worthy sons of warrior sires do ne'er forget their
    birth,
And some of us are proud to own the noblest of the
    earth,—
The true heroic spirit lives that never knew defeat,—
Who fought and won, who sometimes fell, but never
    could retreat.

God bless the Queen, the Prince of Wales, and all the
    Royal line!
May England's star, ascendant still, forever onward
    shine,
As shine it must and will so long as right and truth
    are free,
And Britain, undisputed, owns the Empire of the Sea.

God Bless Her Majesty Queen Victoria.

(AN ACROSTIC.)

GOD bless thee, and thy bannered host!
Of whom it ever has been said,
Died "like true heroes, at their post."

But oftener far to victory led,
Like those of whom we proudly boast,
Engaged the foe, but left them dead!
Such may thy soldiers ever be,
Sons of a knightly chivalry.

Hail, noble Queen! Ye gallant corps,
Engage with cannon's deafening roar,
Resound th' acclaim from shore to shore.

May God still hear our nation's prayer,
And give long life to thee and thine,
Justice and truth preserve thine heir,
Enabling him to live and shine,
Star-like, when other lights decline:
The bright exemplar which a prince should be,
Yielding delight to heaven, to earth, and thee.

Queen, mother of proud nations! Yet
United all in fealty true,
Each in thy crown a jewel set,
Each lending its peculiar hue,
Not rivals, but a blending true.

2

Victoria, Queen and Empress both !
India smiles beneath thy sway.
Canada, in loving troth,
Toasts her Queen this happy day.
On every flagstaff, mast, and tower,
Run up and floating in the breeze,
Is the "old flag" of that great power
All own as EMPRESS OF THE SEAS !

Dominion Day.

WE bask in the sunshine of freedom to-day,
And sing "Our Dominion forever !"
United to each and to England, we pray
The changes of time may ne'er sever.
In ages to come may the men of our land
Unfurl the "old flag" to the breeze;
For union and England unflinchingly stand—
For England, the Queen of the Seas.

CHORUS.

As years roll past we will still stand fast,
No foe the tie shall sever;
But, true to England's throne, fly the flag we're
proud to own,
And the maple leaf forever !

Old England is ours, with her glorious array
   Of names which " Old Time " has made hoary ;
The warrior chiefs of antiquity grey,
   Who each have their halo of glory.
Her hist'ry is full of the noble and great,
   Her heroes are many and grand,
Who laid down their lives at the call of the State,
   In battles on sea and on land.

They died not in vain ; in defence of the right
   A Wolfe and a Nelson don't perish.
As victors they fell in the thick of the fight :
   Their mem'ry we ever shall cherish.
Lord Nelson to-day stirs the heart of the tar ;
   Brave Wolfe and the thousands so slain
Inspire with fresh courage the vet'rans of war
   To deeds of like valour again.

We share in their honours, their history, their fame,
   Their prestige and power as a nation ;
Our birthright as Britons we fearlessly claim,
   Not sever'd from war's obligation.
For should there arise any cause for our aid,
   Or foes try to rend us apart,
Our best blood would answer the first appeal made,
   For Canada's true at the heart.

Some of us are noisy—in speech somewhat free ;
   Yet, count him a foe that would sever—

, As subjects of Britain most loyal are we,
  And wish to remain so forever.
On Confederation we somewhat rely,
  By mutual concessions to live;
And from one another we're hoping to buy
  Whatever each Province can give.

Our notions of trade, even crude tho' they look,
  Have brought out this point, in our thinking,
'Tis better to lead the horse out to the brook,
  Than cart all his water for drinking.
As England receives all our surplus of food, .
  To feed all her thousands, 'tis clear,
'Twould give us less trouble, and do us more good,
  To have them located out here.

To this end our people have voted N.P.,
  To give manufactures protection,
And thus do we hope by industry to see
  The last of hard times and dejection;
When Canada, great, but not standing alone,
  And union a realized fact,
Shall form a grand outpost to strengthen the throne,
  And keep our allegiance intact.

The Men We Want.*

WE want the men of iron nerve,
    Of dauntless heart, of thews like steel,
Who keep their courage in reserve,
    Determined that the foe shall feel
The force of patriotic ire
That strongest burns when under fire.

Who love their country, and the name
    Of Britain as their proudest boast,
Who feel their valour all aflame
    When enemies are off the coast,
Or red rebellion lifts its hand
To break the peace of fatherland.

True-hearted men, who dare to make
    A sacrifice, however dear,
Who put their very lives at stake,
    Whose love of home expels all fear
And makes them feel heroic brave
In prospect of a soldier's grave.

Men who inherit some renown
    Of valiant deed or nation's pride,
Whose fathers, it may be, laid down
    Their lives like Wolfe, yet victors died
Who when he fell was told " They fly,"
" Thank God ! I am content to die."

* Written at the time of the North-West Rebellion, 1885.

Men whose prophetic souls can see
   The fruit of Time's maternal throe,
The grander nation yet to be,
   Of which we are the embryo;
And with this thought their souls aflame,
Do deeds that make a nation's fame.

Men who in righteousness will lay
   The State's foundations broad and strong,
Whose acts will bear the light of day,
   Who have no faith in chartered wrong,
But recognize, where'er they be,
Men have *their* rights as well as *we.*

Men who will keep our statutes free
   From partial laws—a free state's ban;
Men who will say—and, saying, mean—
   They own the brotherhood of man;
But granted that, to each secure
The wealth his skill and thrift procure.

God grant us men like these to bring
   Us through the crisis now at hand,
And men—unborn as yet—shall sing
   Their praises, and be proud to hand
Their names with tenderest memories down,
Each wearing an immortal crown.

Our Fair Dominion.

THE VOLUNTEERS' WAR SONG, No. 1.

TUNE—"Marching Through Georgia."

THE bugle sounds a call to arms! our gallant corps
    reply :
We're ready for the great North-West; we'll make the
    rebels fly.
Hurrah for Canada our home! we'll fight until we die,
    To keep intact our fair Dominion.

CHORUS.

Hurrah! hurrah! for Britain's old renown;
Hurrah! hurrah! for country, Queen and Crown;
Tho' Fenian hordes with Riel may join, we'll put
    rebellion down,
    And keep intact our fair Dominion.

Shall we, whose sires have fought and won on many
    a hard-fought field,
Shall we, with craven fears impelled, our fair posses-
    sions yield ?
Nay! We will fight with all our might, and trust in
    God our shield,
    To keep intact our fair Dominion.

We are the heirs of wealth untold, from East to
    Western sea,
And proud that we, of all earth's sons, are freest of
    the free.
Already dawns the morning of the future yet to be,
      The glory of our fair Dominion.

The hoary Past, the Future, too, our patriot love in-
    spires,
And swells with pride each loyal heart, increasing our
    desires
To prove that we are worthy sons of noble, valiant
    sires,
      Who handed down our fair Dominion.

All honour to the noble men who go at Duty's call,
They leave to us a precious charge—their wives and
    children small—
'Tis ours to see no needless tears shall in their absence
    fall,
      To bring reproach on our Dominion.

Toronto's Welcome Home.

No PEN or pencil can portray
The joy our city feels to-day.
'Mid flags and banners, streamers gay,
   Choice words and apt quotations,
Shakespearean and Byronic lore,
And mottoes we have seen before,
From house and arch and busy store,
   In happiest variations.

One here invites the veteran ranks
From marches to fantastic pranks;
Another says, "Accept our thanks,"
   You've earned it of the nation ;
Another, with extended hand,
Cries "Bully Boys," ye noble band
Of brave defenders of our land,
   Welcome with acclamation.

The sharpened wit of butcher boys
Apt figures from their trade employs,
And wit adds spice to all our joys:
   It tones our exultation,
And makes us of our city feel
Most justly proud, except where Riel
Is hung in effigy ;—Ah, weel,
   He needs commiseration.

Where'er we go " Batoche " is seen
Embowered in arch of fadeless green,
With " Cut Knife," " Fish Creek," in between,
　　Sharing the honored station.
No rivalry at all appears,
The words " Queen's Own " and " Grenadiers "
Invite and share alike our cheers
　　And warmest admiration.

A thousand streamers " Welcome " bear,
Ten thousand flags in color fair,
Unite with all who gladly wear,
　　Mottoes for the occasion ;
A hundred thousand throats proclaim,
With twice that number eyes—aflame
With looks of love no tongue can name—
　　" Accept this grand ovation."

Toronto's Welcome to her Volunteers Home from the War.

Welcome, fathers, lovers, brothers !
　　Heroes not afraid to die,—
Loving wives, sweethearts and mothers,
　　Laughing, weeping, welcome cry.

Nobly have you served your nation,
　　Nobly have you borne the strain ;
Listen to the acclamation :
　　Welcome, patriots, home again !

Bravely have you fought each battle,
   Never once did courage fail ;
Steady, cool, amid the rattle
   And the ping of deadly hail.

Onward marching, forward rushing,
   Charging with resistless might ;
Strong positions taking—pushing
   Out the foe 'mid fiercest fight.

Cool, when comrades fought no longer,
   But lay wounded on the field ;
Brave, when death, sometimes the stronger,
   Forced the dauntless heart to yield.

Brave were ye who faced the foemen !
   Not less brave the noble corps,
Who, with touch like that of woman,
   From the field the wounded bore.

Saving life by quick appliance
   Of the means by skill devised ;
Bidding death meanwhile defiance,
   Danger scarcely realized.

Honoured heroes, worn by marches,
   Long and arduous, o'er the plain,
Welcome ! with triumphal arches,
   Welcome to our hearts again !

Welcome! Let the joy-bells tell it;
  Welcome! Let the cannons roar:
Let the flags and banners wave it
  From each flagstaff, house and store.

Welcome! Let the trumpets blow it;
  Welcome to the brave and true,
Welcome! Let each bright face show it;—
  Thank God, mourners are but few.

But for those to-day in sadness,
  We have feelings deep, unseen;
And in all this joy and gladness,
  Keep their loved ones' memory green.

And we pray, God bless the weeping,
  War-bereft, fond hearts to-day;
Thinking of their dear ones sleeping,
  Crowned with laurel wreaths and bay.

They have passed beyond the portal,
  Leaving something more than name;—
Heroism is immortal;
  They have won a deathless fame.

Welcome, fathers, lovers, brothers!
  Heroes not afraid to die.
Loving wives, sweethearts and mothers,
  Laughing, weeping, welcome cry.

An Ode to Virtue.

I.

VIRTUE—white-robed, angelic—how shall I,
In words befitting, sing thy lofty praise?—
Thou first of graces to adorn mankind,
Thou fount and spring of Eden's bliss and ours.
When God creation crowned with Eve's fair form,
He set thee regnant in their loyal hearts.
Nor wert thou then estranged on earth to dwell,
For Eden's bowers were as Heaven's outer court,
Where they could walk in unrestrainèd love,
And hear sweet music trilling through the spheres.
Harmonious Nature all so smoothly ran,
Earth was enriched, and Heaven well pleased with man.

II.

Short-lived thy kingdom; yet methinks I see
The peerless pair, and in their matchless eyes
An empyrean depth of tranquil blue:
A sea pacific, yet unswept by storms—
Attractive index of soul-purity.
Their breath as incense-spices of Ceylon;
Their thoughts, when voiced, as ecstasy of praise;
Their senses quick, their vision clear and strong,
Beholding far, as on a closer view,
The gorgeous splendours of this new-made world—
Each sense replete, full-orbed, from Nature's store.
With God their friend, how easy to adore!

III.

At eventide with thee they softly walked
Through groves of beauty, or in bowers reclined,
When Helias fair was sinking in the west,
And zephyr breezes toyed with perfumed flowers,
Till heavy laden, they could scarcely move,
But gently clinging to the wings of night,
Sought out the pair and kissed them to repose.
Beneath the snowy folds of innocence,
How sweet they sleep, and how refreshed they rise !
Their smiles as radiant as the blushing morn ;
Their souls, attuned, communion rapt enjoy,
E'er they resume fair Eden's sweet employ.

IV.

How blest were they with thee their constant guest,
And this fair world their pure Elysian home !
For sentient beings what could more suffice ?
Their every sense its full fruition found,
While rich supplies, more ample than their needs,
Inviting hung, nor could they wish for more.
Wisdom Divine imposed but one restraint :
A small denial where profusion reigned,—
A test of love, by true obedience shown,
That they might win thereby a richer crown,
A right to claim thee, Virtue, as their own,
And vie with angels serving near the throne.

V.

Perfection theirs—what more could love bestow?
Their heaven was here, their round of bliss complete.
For them what else remained no man can tell.
Translation hence in deep conjecture lies.—
Alas! alas! the serpent Eve allured,
And doubt infused where simple trust had reigned.
She, all unconscious, opened ear and heart,
Nor once suspected Sin stood at the door,
And, e'er aware or apprehending all,
To Adam gave, and he, beholding, ate.
When lo! Sin, hideous, stood revealed, and they,
Aghast, discovered thou hadst fled away.

The Boat Race on the Thames.

BRAVE OARSMAN! I had almost vowed
That I would no more speak aloud
  On things aquatic;
But thou hast conquered my reserve,
And thrilled again my heart and nerve
  With joy ecstatic.

In fancy's eye I see the strand,
Where eager, well-dressed thousands stand,
  All expectation;
And as I look them in the face,
I see there men of every race
  And every nation.

The French, vivacious, sprightly, gay;
The German, ponderous, heavy clay,
          Square built and massive;
Persians and Greeks from sunny skies,
And Chinamen with almond eyes,
          Silent and passive.

Russians and Turks, Albanians fair,
And Nubians black as jet, are there,
          Idle spectators;
And boisterous groups outside the crowd—
Of all sorts—dialectic, loud,
          Rude speculators.

The proud aristocrat is there,
Who meets us with a vacant stare
          That shuns the masses.
Perhaps he may have learned the trick
From some poor harmless lunatic
          With gold-rimmed glasses.

True gentlemen we often meet,
Whose presence is as great a treat
          As Hanlan's rowing.
We feel they, too, have won their place
By tact and skill and native grace
          Beyond men's showing.

Foremost amid the throng we see
The cream of bad society,
          The pinchbeck swell;

The pearl-washed face devoid of shame,
With passion-kindled eye aflame
    With fires of hell.

John Bull, however, plain John Bull,
Is there, and wants to see the pull
    Between his children;
His honest face, so rubicund,
In spite of all the punning punned,
    Has smiles bewildering.

I like him more than I can tell;
His rotund form becomes him well—
    His corporation
Is index of an easy mind,
Content, wealth, ease, I call combined
    Self-admiration.

Our friends from Scotland, and the Isle
That we call—sister! Do not smile—
    She's just now frisky;
Intoxicated, we may say,
By madcap speeches—everyway
    Far worse than whiskey.

Well, Pat is here to see the sights,
In fun and mischief he delights,
    And wit uproarious.
Aside) "I wish," says he, "our ship of Shtate
Could shlip away as clane and nate
    From Queen Victorious.

3

(*Aloud*) " Bc jabers, how the fellow pulls !
(*Aside*)   Myself would like to use the sculls
     Of Politicians.
   Bedad, I think I'd take the prize,
   Gladstone and Dizzy soon would *rise*
     To *high* positions.

   "Her Majesty ! God bless her sowl !
   I'd put her under mild controwl
     Upon a pension !
   Landlords I'd send to Isle of Skye,
   Or to a place not quite so high,
     I will not mention.

(*Aloud*) " Bravo for Ireland ! Hanlan's won.
(*Aside*)   I wish the work was as well done
     On College Green."
   "Hist, Pat !" a comrade says.   " Beware,
   There's a detective, I declare ! "
(*Aloud*)   " God save the Queen.

   "The big Australian's fairly bate,
   Och, Hanlan does his rowing nate ;
     Just hear them cheer him.
   Three lengths ahead ! and easy, too,
   And Trickett all that he could do,
     Could not get near him."

True Heroism.

WE honour the men who when guns gleam afar,
  And musketry rattles with death-dealing hail,
Are fearless in conflict, successful in war ;
  But honours thus won make the wearer turn pale.

The victor is stained with the blood of the foe,
  His deeds of cool daring are told with a sigh,
His rifle has flashed out its message of woe,
  And deluged with tears many a love-kindled eye.

His sword has cleaved hearts that were true to their
    core,
  And dashed out the hopes of the loved and the
    brave.
He conquered ! But oh, he remembers the gore
  That flowed in a stream from the wounds that he
    gave !

The look of that eye as it flashed in its pain,
  Then glazed into death as his sword was withdrawn,
In dreams of fierce battle he sees it again,
  And waking with joy greets the hour of the dawn.

We honour these men—losing sight of the slain—
  Who fell as their foemen in battle array ;
We honour the man who, on Neptune's domain,
  Has won the world's honours and wears them to-day.

All honour to these ! Yes ! But what of the men
  Whose deeds of cool daring, in fire and in flood,
Have saved precious lives, yes, again and again ?
  For these, can we say we have done what we could ?

The brave fellows, thrilled with humanity's cry,
  Have plunged in the waters or rushed through the
    flame,
And quick to the rescue to save life or die,
  Are heroes who never need blush at the name.

Yet where are their honours ? We dole out our thanks,
  As if every word were a diamond at least;
Then bid them again take their place in the ranks,
  While others less worthy we pension and feast.

To My Own Loved Wife.

THY FACE, dear one, is not so round
    As twenty years ago ;
Thine eyes have lost their depths profound
    Of twenty years ago.
The vision comes before me now,
The sweetly calm, unfurrowed brow,
My peerless bride, my darling thou,
    Of twenty years ago.

The merry laugh, the winsome smile
    Of twenty years ago;
The coy, unconscious, maiden guile
    Of twenty years ago.
The springing step, the easy grace,
The contour fair of form and face,
From memory Time can ne'er erase
    Thee—twenty years ago.

Tho' beauty fades, I love thee more
    Than twenty years ago;
And were we single, I'd adore
    As twenty years ago.
Tho' silver is among thy hair,
Thy face and form to me are fair,
Tho' well I know they can't compare
    With twenty years ago.

Thy cheek has lost the rosy hue
    Of twenty years ago,
But well I know thy heart is true
    As twenty years ago.
And I with pride to thee confess,
    As to my heart thy form I press,
I love thee, dearest, none the less
    Than twenty years ago.

Our Little One that Died.

I THINK I see our baby boy.
　　Our first love's pledge was he—
With bright, blue eyes, a fount of joy
　　To dear mamma and me.
I think I see him even yet,
　　His look of conscious pride;
Tho' years have passed, we can't forget
　　Our little one that died.
　　　　Ah! no; we never can forget
　　　　　Our little one that died.

His chubby little hands and feet,
　　The dimples in his cheek,
His cunning look, his smile so sweet,
　　His first attempts to speak.
The winning ways of our loved pet
　　Keep memory well supplied;
Tho' years have passed, we can't forget
　　Our little one that died.
　　　　Ah! no; we never can forget
　　　　　Our little one that died.

We laid him in his earthy bed
　　When flowers were blooming fair;
And many a bitter tear we've shed
　　Since we have laid him there.
His little toys, we have them yet,
　　Laid tenderly aside;

Tho' years have passed we can't forget
   Our little one that died.
     Ah! no; we never can forget
       Our little one that died.

Blighted Hopes.

A SOLILOQUY.

ALAS! how transient earthly joys!
   How fleeting ours have been!
Our fairest promise death destroys,
   Long e'er the fruit is seen.

And yet thou hast not lived in vain,
   If I can school my heart
To trust in God; we'll meet again
   Where death can never part.

But oh! 'tis hard.   My memory turns
   To every dear delight
Thy love supplied.   My fond heart yearns
   For thee, both day and night!

I never see a manly face,
   But thought returns to thee;
Thy memory Time can ne'er efface,
   Long tho' the parting be.

True as the needle to the pole,
　My heart shall ever prove ;
One image only fills my soul,—
　'Tis thine, departed love.

My heart is widowed ere a bride !
　The bud will never bloom.
Love's nectar'd cup is dashed aside,
　And broken on thy tomb.

Farewell ! until we meet again,
　Beneath heaven's vault serene,
Where sickness, parting, death or pain
　Shall no more intervene.

Nature's Answer to Ingersoll.

" No God ! " the proud blasphemer cries,
And upward turns his flashing eyes
　　To heaven's empyrean blue.
And as he looks, each distant star
Sends down the answer from afar—
　　" Thy blasphemy's untrue.

" Behold our hosts !　Canst thou opine
Who gave to each his orbit line,
　　Through trackless fields of space ;

Caused all harmoniously to move,
Some lower down, some far above,
    Yet each one keep his place?

" All men admit that there are laws
  Which we obey.   Whence then the cause
    Of order's gentle rule?
All nature feels the sweet constraint,   ·
Yet not a whisper of complaint
    Except from man, the fool!

" Behold the flowerets at thy feet;
  Who gave to them their odours sweet,
    Their colours passing fair?
Each petal, pistil, stamen, flower,
Wisdom reveals and wondrous power,
    And love shines everywhere.

" Here means adjusted to their ends,
  Suggest a mind that far transcends
    The finite in its scope.
Research has failed, as yet, to show
What gives the luscious scents that flow
    From rose and heliotrope.

" Is it the soil?   Nay, we have seen,
  The scentless growing in between   ·   ·
    (The Portulacca bright),
While close beside, Narcissus fair
Breathed out its sweetness on the air,
    Throughout the livelong night.

" Hast thou observed the feathered tribe,
And art thou able to describe
  The causes that conspire
To give their plumage every shade,
Not one of which the sun can fade
  With his perennial fire ?

" One feather from the peacock shows
A mystery, canst thou that disclose ?
  Mark well its fair design—
Behold that blue, and bronze, and gold,
Distinctive each ! Canst thou unfold
  This chemistry divine ?

" Whence came the species that we see,
That throng the air, the land, the sea,
  Canst thou, earth's wise one, say ?
Some live on insects, some on seed,
While some on foulest carrion feed.
  ' Instinct !' what is it, pray ?

" Thou, like a screech-owl of the night,
All eye, yet blinded by the light,
  Canst thou this problem solve ?
Came first the egg, bird, tree or seed ?
From whence did men and beasts proceed,
  Or how did they evolve ?"

The Heroes of Senegal.

" STAND by to lower the boat !" the captain cried.
  " It is our only chance ; for I can see
Our labouring ship is too severely tried,
  And must succumb to this tremendous sea."
It was their only chance ; for three long days
  And nights of dread alarm had passed, while he,
The captain, and his crew had tried all ways
  To save his ship, the French brig *St. Pierre.*
She, from the Isle of Bourbon homeward bound
  With precious cargo, had, beside her crew,
One family of four—Madame Lachaux,
  Her son, and two black servants, faithful, true.
Scarce was the captain's order given, when lo !
  With startled fears, her son in fond embrace,
Forth she assayed upon the deck to go,
  And, trembling, met the captain face to face.
Deep draped in mourning, and with eye upturned,
  As if in mute appeal, one moment stood,
Then, with a calmness only few have learned,
  Said, " Fear not, captain, for our God is good."
Brave heart !—but late a moment overcome,—
  No fear she feels ; calm and serene her brow,
As if some messenger from heaven had come,
  Assuring her of perfect safety now.

And while her servants help the ship's tired hands
  To launch the boat, her thoughts are far away :—

Her daughter's new-made grave in burning sands,
   And with the husband she had sent away,
His shattered health to gain in southern France.
   And yet 'mid such sad thoughts as these she feels
Her hope of joining him is no mere chance;
   For Faith's pure light a future bright reveals.
Instinctively she dreads the foaming sea,
   Yet, Peter-like, she hears the Master's voice;
And, scarcely knowing how it yet shall be,
   Yields to His will as tho' it were her choice.
Brave Captain Pickard gently lowers her down;
   While in his arms the negro, brave Achille,
Bears Master Henri, while a threat'ning frown
   Comes o'er the crew to see the boat thus fill.
At last! with all aboard they move away,
   And scarcely clear, when, with a loud report
Of bursting decks, she disappears in spray,
   And leaves the boat alone and far from port.
So crowded is she that they have no room
   To set up sail or ply the needed oar.
The sailors mutter that "'tis certain doom
   With such a load, and they so far from shore,"
And darkly hint "that something must be done,
   Or else they all will sink. Wherefore retain
The useless hands, the lady and her son?
   Cast them adrift; the rest may then remain."

The captain heard their words, and quick as thought
   Felt for his pistols. But the brave Achille

Cried, " Look, massa !   They want to light the boat.
  Pierrot and I will do it.   You sit still.
Swear you will save our mistress and her son,
  And that you'll keep them from all danger free.
We heavier than they both. Now swear." 'Twas done.
  They bid farewell, then plunge into the sea.
Brave fellows ! it was not in vain.   The boat,
  Eased of her load, was bailed ; the oars were plied,
And soon her head to breast the waves was brought,
  And hope revived that they might safely ride
The still tempestuous waves. So passed the night,
  Their only hope the mercy of the Lord.
Next day an English schooner hove in sight,
  Their boat espied, and took them all on board.

A few weeks more and then Madam Lachaux
  Rejoined her husband in his native land,
And in their ramblings visit St. Malo,
  A famed seaside resort.   There on the strand,
With Master Henri playing at their feet,
  They sit and watch the slow receding tide.
With grateful heart he hears his wife repeat
  The tale again, how their brave negroes died.
Absorbed, they muse upon their noble deed,
  And memory links them with the moaning sea.
Of those around they take but little heed,
  Wishing what they suppose could never be.
Yet near them stands a captain talking to
  A gentleman about two men he found.
" Now they are here, I know not what to do ;
  They speak not French, and I am outward bound."

" Where found you them, say you ?" "A bit sou'-west
   Of the Cape, half-dead, clinging to a spar;
And when revived, O how the fellows pressed
   Me to allow them work their passage where
Their mistress lives !   And when they told me all
   About the wreck my heart was touched, and I
Turned from my course, determined that I'd call
   At some French port.   And that's the reason why
I'm in St. Malo, just to leave them here.
   About their mistress, all they seem to know
Is, she was French ; and more, it doth appear,
   From what they say, her name was M. Lachaux."
"And here she is !" cried Madam. "Where's my friends ?
   Let me their deed requite.   They quelled the strife
Of angry men, and to defeat their ends
   Plunged headlong in the sea to save my life."

One half-hour more each was to each restored,
   'Mid cordial greetings and fast-falling tears.
The very best St. Malo could afford
   Was not too good for these Senegal peers.*
A handsome present to the captain made
   Marked their esteem of his most gallant deed,
And to the negroes such attention paid
   As grateful hearts aye think befitting meed.
And when in after years, on festive days,
   Young Master Henri bid guests bumpers fill,
He would recount their deed with highest praise,
   And drink the health of Pierrot and Achille.

* Natives of Senegal.

Recollections of Barnard Castle.

LEAVING the busy market place,
Where horses, sheep and cattle stand,
We seek the outskirts of the town
Which bears the grand old ruin's name.
Southward we bend our willing feet,
And as we catch a distant glimpse
Of frowning tower and battlement,
In fancy's eye we see the knights,
Who, armour-clad, keep watch and ward,
When royalty in pomp and state
Held court in Barnard's spacious halls,
When barons proud and courtiers gay.
Crowded the portals every day.
The ramparts high, with one round tower,
Alone remains; we climb the stair
Secret within its ample walls.
Through loop-holed galleries we pass;
Still round and round till we emerge,
Half-blinded with the light of day.
We shade our eyes to view the scene,
And eastward look o'er ruins grey.
'Twas there the stately chapel stood,
Back from the ramparts, sacred now
To ferns and brambles; while the ground,
Rich with the blood of warriors, yields
Her fruit to horticultural art.
Where princes feasted, there the spade

Has done its work; naught now remains
But those far-reaching outer walls,
And this old tower on which we stand.
Beneath we view the dungeon deep
Where royal Barnard three full years
Was kept in chains ere pardon came.
Sick with the horrors we are told
Of barb'rous treatment, rapes and deaths,
Again we seek the open air,
Thankful for peace and sylvan shade.
Hard by us runs the murmuring Tees,
Whose moor-stained waters lashed to foam
Have rushing leaped full many a fall,
And now, at Barnard's rocky feet,
They pour their wealth of rippling song.
Fair, lovely stream!   But erst thou flowed
Incarnadined with warriors' gore,
When Cromwell, proud, victorious, strong,
Beleagured, fought and conquered here.
His guns this ruin wrought.   His men
Those ramparts scaled, and with a shout
That rent the air, "Surrender!" cried.
Yet ere proud Barnard's men fell back,
Full many a noble bit the dust,
And rolled impetuous down the steep
To add his life-blood to the stream—
Already red; for man and beast,
Who fell while fighting at the ford,
Together mingled in the tide.
Behold yon warrior as he falls,

His horse shot dead.   His feet are caught
And hang still in the trappings; see,
His waving plume goes floating down;
His bright cuirass shines through the waves;
He cries, he struggles to get free,
And beats to foam the waters round,
Then, choking, sinks to rise no more.
But hark! The fortunes of the fight
Are, notwithstanding, on his side;
Brave, fearless men have scaled the walls,
And hand to hand have fought their way
Till now the keep is in their hands,
Its brave defenders pris'ners all,
And Cromwell master of the place!

Beautiful England.

O, BEAUTIFUL England! my thoughts love to dwell
Among thy green mountains and scenes I love well;
The home of my childhood is dear still to me—
O, beautiful England! my heart clings to thee.

'Tis long since I wandered where fancy beguiled,
Among thy deep valleys, when I was a child:
Those days of past pleasure remember'd shall be—
O, beautiful England! my heart clings to thee.

Thy flora so lovely, thy shrubs rich and rare,
Thy landscapes of beauty surpassingly fair;

4

Such lawns and surroundings I ne'er hope to see—
O, beautiful England! my heart clings to thee.

The homes of thy nobles, how lovely they stand,
Like pictures of beauty adorning the land,
Replete with art treasures to which all are free—*
O, beautiful England! my heart clings to thee.

When tempted by fortune, she led me to stray
Across the wide sea to this land far away;
But fond recollections abide still with me—
O, beautiful England! my heart clings to thee.

Here nature, though kindly, must yield to the clime—
Our scenes are wild grandeur, approaching sublime.
Niagara's thunder is music to me—
Yet, beautiful England! my heart clings to thee.

* Many of the finest mansions in England are open to the public one day in the week.

FINIS.

www.ingramcontent.com/pod-product-compliance
Lightning Source LLC
Chambersburg PA
CBHW021545270326
41930CB00008B/1366